# THE STANGE PARNERSHIP

# OF

# GEORGE ALEXANDER McGUIRE

# AND

# MARCUS GARVEY

## MORE WILDSIDE CLASSICS

*Dacobra, or The White Priests of Ahriman*, by Harris Burland
*The Nabob*, by Alphonse Daudet
*Out of the Wreck*, by Captain A. E. Dingle
*The Elm-Tree on the Mall*, by Anatole France
*The Lance of Kanana*, by Harry W. French
*Amazon Nights*, by Arthur O. Friel
*Caught in the Net*, by Emile Gaboriau
*The Gentle Grafter*, by O. Henry
*Raffles*, by E. W. Hornung
*Gates of Empire*, by Robert E. Howard
*Tom Brown's School Days*, by Thomas Hughes
*The Opium Ship*, by H. Bedford Jones
*The Miracles of Antichrist*, by Selma Lagerlof
*Arsène Lupin*, by Maurice LeBlanc
*A Phantom Lover*, by Vernon Lee
*The Iron Heel*, by Jack London
*The Witness for the Defence*, by A.E.W. Mason
*The Spider Strain and Other Tales,* by Johnston McCulley
*Tales of Thubway Tham,* by Johnston McCulley
*The Prince of Graustark*, by George McCutcheon
*Bull-Dog Drummond*, by Cyril McNeile
*The Moon Pool*, by A. Merritt
*The Red House Mystery*, by A. A. Milne
*Blix*, by Frank Norris
*Wings over Tomorrow,* by Philip Francis Nowlan
*The Devil's Paw*, by E. Phillips Oppenheim
*Satan's Daughter and Other Tales,* by E. Hoffmann Price
*The Insidious Dr. Fu Manchu*, by Sax Rohmer
*Mauprat*, by George Sand
*The Slayer and Other Tales,* by H. de Vere Stacpoole
*Penrod (Gordon Grant Illustrated Edition)*, by Booth Tarkington
*The Gilded Age*, by Mark Twain
*The Blockade Runners*, by Jules Verne
*The Gadfly*, by E.L. Voynich

*Please see www.wildsidepress.com for a complete list!*

# THE STANGE PARNERSHIP
## OF
## GEORGE ALEXANDER McGUIRE
## AND
## MARCUS GARVEY

by
Bishop Karl Prüter

Copyright © 1986 by Karl Prüter

All rights reserved. No part of this book my be reproduced in any form without the expressed written consent of the publisher.

**THE STANGE PARNERSHIP
OF
GEORGE ALEXANDER McGUIRE
AND
MARCUS GARVEY**

This edition published in 2006 by Wildside Press, LLC.
www.wildsidepress.com

## EARLY LIFE

Geroge Alexander McGuire was born on the 26th of March, 1866, in Antigua, Bristish West Indies. He was the son of Edward Henry McGuire and Henrietta (George). His parents were determined that their son would receive a Christian upbringing and a good education. In the British West Indies Blacks were restricted in many ways, but if they could find the means, they were not prevented from obtaining an education. The McGuires knew that education was the only avenue to success and they encouraged George and made sacrifices in order that he might improve his mind. They helped him acquire the skills and education to become a physician, a surgeon, and a minister.

He graduated from Mico College, Antigua in 1886, the Theological Seminary at St. Thomas in 1888, and he received his M.D. from Jefferson Medical College in Boston in 1910. To become trained in two fields is unusual for persons of any race, but considering the economic condition of most West Indian Blacks in the latter part of the 19th century, it was a truly remarkable achievement. When the African Orthodox Church was organized a decade later, this example of McGuire's would be copied by other leaders of the Church.

While pursuing his education he found his life's partner and married Ada Eliza Roberts of Antigua on December 20, 1892. He began his career in the Protestant Episcopal Church and served parishes in the United States from 1888 until 1913. After 1913 he and his wife returned to the British West Indies where he served not only as a priest in the Protestant Episcopal Church, but also as a family physician.

Father George McGuire had an opportunity to minister to both the physical and spiritual needs of his parishoners. His dual role, gave him an opportunity to study and to understand the conditions under which they lived and worked. British Colonialism of the early twentieth century could be described as benevolent, but it was, none the less, colonialism. The Negroes had few opportunities for advancement, although as I have pointed out, they were permitted to acquire an education, if they could find the means. There were many people, both black and white, interested in improving the lot of the Negro. McGuire was to become closely involved with the most colorful and practical of them, Marcus Garvey. Garvey was born in Jamaica in 1887, and in 1914 he organized the Universal Negro Improvement Association which very quickly built a membership of millions. It had one aim and that was to improve the status of Negroes through the united efforts of Negroes everywhere. Garvey believed in self help, or to put it even more accurately, he believed that only by his own efforts, could the Negro improve his lot, that was by pursuing a medical career or a clerical career, and McGuire chose both of them. But he couldn't and wouldn't ignore the plight of members of his race that lacked either the talent or the opportunities that he had had. He not only joined the Universal Negro Improvement Association but quickly worked his way in the organization and became a right hand for its leader, Marcus Garvey.

McGuire had, by any standard, a successful career in the Protestant Episcopal Church. Before entering Jefferson Medical College, he had been considered for the post of Suffragan Bishop of Arkansas. He declined and gave as his reason his desire to study medicine. He also may have rejected the offer because of the subordinate role of a suffragan bishop. Such a position would not greatly advance the cause of the Negro in America. After his graduation from medical school he served at St. Bartholomew's Episcopal Church in Cambridge, Massachusetts. He remained there for six years and then he became the Secretary of the Commission for work among the Colored people under the Board of Missions of the Protestant Episcopal Church. In this position he was able to travel throughout the country and he was easily the best known man of color in the Episcopal Church.

He did not remain long at this post because like many West Indians, he longed to return to the island where he was born.

He desired to build a church in his hometown of Sweets, and he spent the next six years of his life in building, not only the edifice, but also the spiritual strength of the congregation it housed. These were happy years for McGuire but as he became more and more involved with Marcus Garvey's United Negro Improvement Association, he found himself increasingly dissatisfied with what he saw as a second class role for the Negro in the Protestant Episcopal Church.

He returned to the United States and began to consider the possibility of an independent and Negro Episcopal Church. After talking with the Reformed Episcopalians, and a number of independent parishes he began a small mission on his own. On September 2, 1921 he was in the Church of the Good Shepherd in New York City attending a meeting of an independent group of Black Episcopal clergy. The meeting resulted in the formation of the Afraican Orthodox Church, and while meeting in synod, it elected Fr. George Alexander McGuire to be its first bishop.

As former Episcopalians, Apostolic Succession was important to the new Church. They could hardly go to Canterbury for they were regarded as schismatics by the Anglican Church. Like other similar groups before them, they approached a mainline Orthodox Church; in this case, the Russian Orthodox Church in America. They soon discovered that the Russian Church would not consecrate a bishop for a body which intended to remain independent. Yet, having just declared their independence from one White dominated Church, they were not going to give up their independence to another. Although, it was not their first choice, they turned to the American Catholic Church, headed by Archbishop Joseph Rene Vilatte. Bishop Frederick Lloyd, who was Villate's suffragan, prefered that the new body become part of the American Catholic Church, but McGuire and his people were adamant. They wanted a Negro Church. At this point in his life, Archbishop Vilatte had given up his dream of building a large jurisdiction and saw his role as providing the Apostolic Succession where it was sought and where it might advance the gospel. After a quarrel with Lloyd, he proceeded on September 29, 1921, with Bishop Carl A. Nybladh to consecrate Dr. McGuire in the Church of Our Lady of Good Death in Chicago. From this point one, the Church was to become the main focus in the life of George Alexander McGuire. But it was not the only activity, for his work in the Universal Negro Improvement Association of the World, would demand many of his working hours and much of his creativity and leadership. Because of his great interest in the work of the Association and because much of the early membership of the African Orthodox Church was drawn from the movement, we ought to look at the contribution of Marcus Garvey and the association which he founded.

## THE UNIVERSAL NEGRO IMPROVEMENT ASSOCIATION

Founded on August 1, 1914 by Marcus Garvey, the Universal Negro Improvement Association became the largest and the most influential organization in the early part of the twentieth century for the purpose of improving the lot of the Negro. Garvey was born on August 17, 1887 at St. Ann's Bay, Jamaica, B.W.I., to Marcus and Sarah Garvey. His father was a stonemason and was respected in the community for his learning. Marcus Junior's mother was a deeply religious woman who was determined that her son should be a leader and a good Methodist.

Garvey's interest in the Church was largely motivated by his interest in the style of its preachers. He attended regularly in his teens and paid a great deal of attention, more to how the preacher spoke, than to what he said. He also took elocution lessons from a number of teachers. One who had great influence upon him was The Rev. Joseph Robert Love, a Protestant Episcopal priest and a physician. It was he, who as editor of the Jamica ADVOCATE first used the slogan, "Africa for the Africans" which would also become the slogan for the Universal Negro Improvement Association. Father Love not only influenced Garvey's thought, but he inspired Garvey in his choice of journalism as his profession. Garvey apprenticed himself to the profession at the age of 12 and from 1903 until 1907 he worked for a Kingston newspaper. When he lost his job as the result of a printers' strike, he worked for a while as a government printer and then decided to edit and publish the Watchman. It is not easy to finance a newspaper and the Watchman soon failed. Since he was blacklisted as a result of the strike, he found it difficult to make a living in Jamaica. He left the island when he was twenty-three and went to Costa Rica where his uncle helped him get a job as timekeeper on a plantation run by the United Fruit Company. He was profoundly disturbed by the labor conditions which his fellow West Indians had to endure. He went to the British Consul to protest and was met with indifference. Once again, he went to the printed page and founded a pa paper, La Nacionale, which like The Watchman, failed because of insufficient financing. In Panama he found similar working conditions for the West Indian Blacks, and again, he founded a newspaper, this time La Prensa, but it met the same fate as the two previous ventures.

Since officials in Costa Rica and Panama seemed not to care what happened to West Indian Blacks, he thought that the Governor of Jamaica would show an interest. He returned to Jamaica and quickly discover that His Majesty's representative was no more concerned about his Jamaican subjects of color than the officials in Central America. The government's attitude was that the Negroes had gone to Central America voluntarily and if they didn't like it they could always return to Jamaica. So in 1912, he decided that perhaps if he went to the source of democracy, the Empire's Capitol City of London, he might meet with more success. It was here that Garvey saw clearly what he would have to do to help his race improve the lot of Negroes in the world.

While in London he read Booker T. Washington's <u>Up From Slavery</u> and drew some conclusions that were to shape the future of Marcus Garvey and for millions of Blacks. He was impressed by the achievements of Washington, but he was also finding that in London, the seat of the Empire, there was no one who could speak for the Blacks. The Black man had no government, no army, and no king or kingdom. To rely upon the benevolance of the White man was both uncertain and demeaning. In London he was meeting Black men from all over the world and it was intellectually stimulating. Certain ideas were being expressed by by Blacks from the four corners of the earth. Anticolonialism was being stimulated by the education to which colonial citizens of every race and hue were being exposed in the British educational system. Blacks and other colonials were seeing the need to maintain their identity and Blacks from all over the world wanted to create unity among the world's Black people.

Once he had organized his own thoughts, he was eager to do whatever was necessary to implement them. He felt that the West Indians, as a group, were in the best position to lead a movement that would not only free Blacks from oppression but would raise them up so that they would be second to no race on earth. He returned to Jamaica in 1914 on the first of August, the anniversary of emancipation in the British West Indies. He immediately set about to organize the Universal Negro Improvement and Conservation Association and African Communities' League. In the future the name would be shortened and referred to as the UNIA. Its principal aims were to provide colleges for the education of the Negro, raise pride in their race, promote commerce and industry, (although the term had not been invented Garvey firmly believe in "green power") and strengthen the imperialism of independent African States." Garvey wanted all the Black colonies in Africa to be free and self governing. In 1914 it was difficult to imagine how it could come about and Garvey's thought was that the existing Negro States might become instruments for the liberation of their neighboring colonial states.

His slogan "One God! One Aim! One Destiny! did not find an immediate acceptance among his fellow West Indian Negroes. The middle class, in particular, did not respond to such candid rhetoric as "Get the kinks out of your mind instead of your hair". Those who imitated Whites and who used hair straighteners, rejected the notion that to think Black it was also helpful to look Black. But Garvey felt Negroes like all other people had to learn to be proud of what and who they were. Again, he did not coin the phrase, "Black is beautiful" but he believed it and taught it.

Garvey had been in correspondence for many years with Booker T. Washington and at this time, Washington was urging him to come to the United States. It was an irrestible appeal because, first of all, Garvey had been profoundly influenced by Washington's book, "Up From Slavery" and he was anxious to meet the man. Other factors had to be the large Negro population in the United States, and that, at least, on paper the United States offered equal opportunity for all. In March of 1916 Garvey sailed for the United States, although his idol and mentor Booker T. Washington had died.

Upon his arrival he began to travel throughout the United States and soon discovered for himself the gulf between the

American ideal and American practice. Negroes had just enthusiastically participated in America's first war abroad and many of them returned very disillusioned They had fought, bled and died but when they returned they had less freedom in their own land than they had in France. They had gone to Europe to fight "barbarism" and returned to a land where they were not safe from lynching and unpremeditated violence.

Garvey looked first at the situation which was deplorable. Blacks were discriminated against in every segment of society and were given only the meanest and poorest paying jobs. Then when he looked at the Negro leadership he was disturbed. He tells of a visit to W. E. B. Du Bois in the offices of the National Association for the Advancement of Colored People and being dumbfounded to find that no Negro was employed there that was truly black in color. One had to be very light skinned in order to work for the number one organization that was working for equal rights for the Negroes. Nothing in their charter said, "Equal rights only for light skinned Negroes" but clearly something had gone awry. To Garvey it was clear. The National Association was made up of both Whites and Negroes and depended for its funding largely on Whites. The Negro leadership was afraid that if a White donor came into the offices he might be turned off if the workers looked "too" black. Garvey felt it was necessary for the Negro to wake up to the fact that

Negroes could better their lot only when they learned to depend upon themselves, their own efforts and their own money.

One of Marcus Garvey's strong points was his willingness to observe and learn. He spent a year in traveling throughout the United States and spoke with every major Negro leader, until he felt he understood the situation for Blacks in the United States. He saw poverty, the repression, and the inequality, but he also saw that the Negro in the United States had managed, in spite of the system, to advance educationally, financially, and socially. The small gains, in spite of the handicaps, convinced Garvey that in America the Negro had an opportunity to move ahead towards full equality and to realize his full potential. He opened a New York office with high hope and it was in this city that he would lead the UNIA for eleven years. He very quickly sparked the imagination of the American Negroes. For one thing, although he was an alien, he spoke out clearly and strongly. He denounced the East St. Louis race riot and attributed it to Black oppression. Negroes in 1917 were not supposed to say such things, and many of his critics pointed out not only that he was a Negro but a foreigner to boot. When the troops returned to America after World War I, Garvey again spoke to their disillusionment. He sounded inflammatory to many of his critics when he said,"The first dying that is to be done by the Black man in the future will be done to

make himself free. And then when we are
finished, if we have any charity to bestow, we may die for the white man. But
as for me, I think I have stopped dying
for him." Garvey was seen by many Whites,
and by some Blacks, as a man to be feared.
But more importantly his fellow Negroes
responded when he said, "I am the equal of
any white man; I want you to feel the same
way. No more fear, no more cringing, no
more sycophantic begging and pleading."

He was also critical of the Black Church
and spoke against its tendency to blame God
for the condition of the Negro. In fact,
he tended to place the blame on the shoulders of the very people who he felt called
to lead. He attributed their condition to
"Sloth, neglect, indifference" and insisted
that "Confidence, conviction, (and) action
will cause us to be free men today."

Marcus Garvey has often been pictured
as a religious cynic who felt it was important that the Negro come out from under
the influence of the church. Garvey did
not have trouble with the church, but he
did not view it uncritically. Sometime
between 1917 and 1919 he was joined by
George Alexander McGuire who was to become his right hand man and who would
address the religious question. To
Garvey it was not a question of whether
the Negro should or should not be religious, for the practical fact of the
matter was that he was, and probably
would always remain so. What concerned
him was the message of the Black Church.

If it told the Negro he was equal to any race, and that his role in the world was to become great in the sight of God, then Garvey would echo "Amen". Both he and McGuire were determined that the Church as well as every other institution in Negro life should get the message that Blacks were not inferior and in the sight of God were equal to any race.

McGuire was given the title of Chaplain-General and he proceeded to do many things for the UNIA that one only did for established churches. He prepared a catechism, and a liturgy and both of these reflected his own Episcopal Faith. He had to walk a tightrope because thousands of clergymen of many faiths were members of the UNIA and would have been disturbed if they felt any particular church or sect were to receive preferement within the organization. As long as no problems resulted from his work, Garvey was content to allow McGuire to continue the work of remolding the theology of the Negro churches, which is what both McGuire and Garvey had set out to do.

Later after McGuire left the Episcopal Church to form the African Orthodox Church they would briefly quarrel. But the quarrel, which we shall consider later, was not over the formation of the African Orthodox Church, but was concerned with its status in the UNIA. Garvey feared that if it was given too large a role in his Association, it might drive out the thousands of Negroes who prefered the

Methodist, Baptist or other Christian denominations or even non-Christian religiona

Marcus Garvey had a following that was numbered in millions. How many actually joined the UNIA is not certain, but in 1919 he claimed two million members, in 1921, four million members and in 1923, he claimed a membership of six million members. It is difficult to check these numbers but in 1925 he had 700 branches in the United States and over 200 outside of the country. Garvey was first of all a preacher and a prophet. His style was that of a Black evangelist and he spoke of the suffering of Jesus Christ and insisted that "Christ died to make men free".

His message was spiritual, but he believed in the social gospel as well. In 1919 he formed the Negro Factories Corporation by asking his followers to buy 200,000 shares of stock at $5.00 per share. The corporation operated grocery stores, restaurants, a printing plant, a laundry, and it manufactured uniforms, hats, shirts, and other items of clothing. Most important it published a newspaper, the <u>Negro World</u>. all the corporation employed over a thousand people. In the same year he created the Black Star Line and with a capitalization of $610,000 he purchased three ships which hauled freight largely to the West Indies for three years, when it had to suspend opperations. Although economically the steamship line failed, it aroused considerable pride in the Negro community. Its failure is not surprising since few Negroes, in the early 1920's, had much experience or expertise in the world of finance and business. When the line failed, many of the investors were disillusioned, but many more remembered that when one of its ships docked in Havana, Philadelphia, Boston or New York, it was greeted by hundreds and sometimes thousands of visitors. As a symbol, the Black Star Line was a great success, and Garvey's message was heard over and over again by the crowds who came to greet the ships. The vision of a united Africa ruled by Negroes was important, but more important was the pride in race that was heard when Garvey spoke and made visible by three old, decrepit, and money losing ships. It must also be remembered that Garvey, at no time, envisioned great numbers of Blacks from the United States or the West Indies returning to Africa. He wanted to take them back to Africa spiritually and in their immagination. He wanted them to be conscious of their roots, take pride in their roots, and in return help the Negroes of Africa to become free of White colonial rule.

Marcus Garvey was loved by millions, but he also had many enemies, particularly among the leaders of Negro organzations which competed with the UNIA for membership. When the Black Star Line went under, financially, there were hints of fraud and financial irregularities. Garvey may have been guilty of mismanagement, and if so, that was hardly criminal. But the courts took a different view and he was sentenced to five years in prison. There were four defendants but he alone was found guilty. On November 18, 1927 President Calvin Coolidge commuted Garvey's sentence which had a bit more than two years to run. He was deported as an undesirable alien and he returned to his native Jamaica. Here he attempted to run the UNIA and was elected to the governing body of Kingston. He found Jamaica too confining and in 1935 he moved to London where he continued to edit and publish his magazine, The Black Man. The publication continued until 1939 when it died, as did so many of his previous publications, from lack of money. A year later Garvey did at the age of fifty-two, in London. He was poor, virtually alone, but he was to be forever remembered as a great leader and one of the first of his race to speak out concerning the necessity and the rightness of "Black Pride".

The Universal Negro Improvement Association which he founded still lives today. It is small and its influence has declined but Garvey is rembered and his message continues. Signficantly, one of the places where his memory is strongest is among the members of the African Orthodox Church. The formation of this Church is viewed by many historians as being a minor event in the history of the UNIA which did not enjoy the full support of Marcus Garvey. Both contentions are debatable, but what is more important that it is one of the few creations of the Garvey movement that continues to live and exert influence today. If Garvey had a few reservations about it, his lieutenant, George Alexander McGuire, had none.

## THE GROWTH OF THE AFRICAN ORTHODOX CHURCH

The position of George McGuire in the UNIA was one that would have satisfied almost any clergyman in America. He was chaplain of an organization of millions in which religion played a very large fole. He had prepared the <u>Universal Negro Ritual</u> and the <u>Universal Negro Catechism.</u> Both books reflected his beliefs and practices. The acceptance of these books by the mebership of the UNIA is remarkable because such a very small percentage of the membership was Episcoplaian. But the support of Marcus Garvey, together with his own personal charisma won acceptace of what became the "civil religion" of the UNIA. There was, some dissent and this concerned Garvey and in 1923 Garvey and McGuire were in open conflict. It was not that Garvey was unsympathetic with what McGuire was doing, but he was anxious not to offend the Methodists, Baptists, Jews, and seculaists who made up the majority of the UNIA membership.

It was a dispute that was healed quickly and for as much as McGuire would have like it, if the African Orthdox

Church became the "official" church of the Universal Negro Improvement Association he was too practical a man to press his case too hard. Further Garvey needed the support and the mind of McGuire and as long as the Association and the Church were seen as separate bodies pursuing some of the same goals, the two men continued to work together.

The idea of an African Orthodox Church had not come to McGuire full blown. It was not long after his ordination in the Episcopal Church that McGuire realized he could not be content with the status of the Negro in that Church. He tried reform from within, but he very quickly realized that the Episcopal Church was not about to consecrate bishops of color and if it did, it would not place them in positions of authority, but rather as suffragan bishops. He next thought in terms of a Negro Episcopal Church which would be a parallel communion to the Protestant Episcopal Church as the African Methodist Church ran parallel to the Methodist Church. He soon saw that while such a move would provide independence it would imply second class status. He next turned to the Reformed Episcopal Church which had a large Negro membership, although it was White run and Whites predominated.

He founded the Church of the Good Shepherd on November 9, 1919 and the congregation came into communion with the Reformed Episcopal Church. However, McGuire soon felt that since his role in the UNIA was so large he could not afford to be identified with a White dominated church. Consequently, he formed the African Episcopal Church in April of 1920 and the Church of the Good Shepherd became the first parish of the new denomination. In March of the next year, he ordained the Rev. Richard Hilton Tobitt, presbyter. Tobitt had formerly been a deacon in the African Methodist Episcopal Church and held a high position in the UNIA.

There were a number of very significant things about the ordination of Rev. Tobitt. First, he was sent to the West Indies as General Missionary by not only the Church but also by the UNIA. Further the UNIA purchased the episcopal robes worn by McGuire at Tobitt's ordination. In all there was an explicit indication that the new church had a special relationship with the UNIA. Perhaps, this marked the beginning of dissent among the other clergy in the UNIA, for Garvey had never purchased, with UNIA funds, vestments for other clergy.

Of course, the ordination of itself raised some questions in many minds, especially in the mind of "Bishop" George McGuire. It was done in the name of the African Episcopal Church, but by any Episcopal standards it fell short of being a valid ordination. The fact was that McGuire was not a true bishop according to Episcopal and Catholic tradition and teachings. He had never been consecrated a bishop by a bishop in

any line of Apostolic Succession. The
Catholic, Orthodox and Anglican Churches
all hold the position that a presbyter,
i.e., a priest, in order to validly per-
form his priestly functions, had to be
ordained in the apostolic succession. The
doctrine is very simple. It holds that
Peter, as first bishop, consecrated
bishops who in turn consecrated bishops
down through the ages. The doctrine con-
tends that every bishop of the Church can
trace his consecration back to Peter
through bishops who inherited his succession. Without such succession no ordination or consecration can be considered
valid.

Thus the ordination of Tobitt is
strange in many respects. Of course,
McGuire did not claim to be a bishop,
although he wore bishop's robes and
ordained a presbyter. It was not until
July 16, 1921 at a synod in Brooklyn, that
he was formally elected bishop. It was at
this point that Mcguire and Garvey quar-
reled and the Negro World published an
editorial stating that the U.N.I.A. favors
all churches, but adopts none as the UNIA
"Church".

But George Alexander McGuire, the
bishop-elect went ahead and on September
18, 1911, at the hands of Archbishop
Joseph Rene Vilatte, he was consecrated
Bishop of the African Orthodox Church.
The name African Orthodox had been agreed
upon at a meeting several weeks earlier at
a synod of the Independent Episcopal

Church which had convened at the Church of the Good Shepherd in Brooklyn. The consecration and the formation of the Church were greeted in the Negro World, but again with a statement disassociating the Church from the UNIA. Although, the Russian Orthodox Church had declined to consecrate McGuire, Bishop Anthony R. F. Hill of that Church participated in the enthronement of the first bishop of the AOC in New York City on the 29 of September 1921.

    It is obvious from the work George McGuire put into the laying of the foundation of the African Orthodox Church that he expected it would become the church of the UNIA. He prepared the "Universal Negro Catechism" and the "Universal Negro Ritual" partially because he was comfortable with the ideas expressed in these works, but also becaue he hoped they would help pave the way for the Church he had envisioned. By whatever name, the "Church Ethiopic" would unite all Negroes in a church they could call their own. When it was clear that there was considerable opposition to the idea within the UNIA, McGuire, not a man to be easily dissuaded went ahead. He believed the African Orthodox Church would attract millions and certainly all those within the UNIA who did not have strong committments to the existing churches and synagogues. That he was disappointed is evident from the address he delievered in August of 1924 at the convention of the Universal Negro Improvement Association. He said that it was "the height of stupidity and self-negation" for Black people to worship a Caucasian deity. He suggested, "Let us start our Negro painters getting busy and supply a black Madonna and a black Christ for the training of our children." McGuire knew Christ and His Mother Mary were Jewish, but he also knew that God and His Son were not "White", "Black", or "Red". Since we cannot portray a colorless God, Christ, or Mary, we tend to think of them as reflections of ourselves. Whites had pictures of Christ and Mary as White, so it was desirable, and even necessary, to provide a Black Christ and a Black Mary for the training of Negro children. As he spoke to the Convention he stood before a backgrop which pictured an Ethiopian Christ and a Black Saint Mary. McGuire asked the delegates to "Erase the White gods from your hearts. We must go back to our own native church and to our God."

McGuire had envisioned a church that would see God as black, and whose leadership would be Black, but would refuse membership to none because of race. He was also anxious that the new Church would possess the Historic Episcopate. At a meeting of the Independent Episcopal Churches on September 2, 1921, at the Good Shepherd Church, the delegates resolved themselves into the first synod of the African Orthodox Church. Several names for the new body were suggested but McGuire's choice was finally agreed upon. At this point in time, he had already begun negotiations with the Russian Orthodox Church. The negotiations failed because McGuire did not wish the African Orthodox Church to be merely a subdivision of the Russian Orthodox Church.

He next turned to the Old Catholic Church of America, headed by Archbishop Joseph Rene Vilatte. It was a church with little prestige, few members and a rather short history. Although Vilatte was not his first choice of consecrators, there was much to recommend Vilatte. Neither Bishop Joseph Vilatte nor the church he represented made any demands upon the new African Orthodox Church or its bishop-elect, George McGuire. We do not know what prompted Vilatte to consecrate McGuire. It was his last consecration and was performed on September 28, 1921 at Our Lady of Good Death in Chicago with Bishop Carl A. Nybladh as co-consecrator. Most probably, Vilatte felt that he had been called to provide the historic episcopate to any ethnic group to which it had been denied by the "establishment". Those who wished the African Orthodox Church well applauded the consecration and saw it as valid regardless of the smallness of Bishop Vilatte's Church and his lack of status. Opponents raised questions regarding the authenticity of his orders and, what they saw, as the pretensions of the new Church and its leadership.

The new Church began with a nucleus of congregations brought to it from the Independent Episcopal Church and grew very rapidly. It claimed congregations in Brooklyn, Pittsburgh, Boston, Nova Scotia, Cuba, Santo Domingo, and very quickly spread to other parts of the West Indies and the United States. In 1924 it was able to reach out to the Continent of Africa through a South African, Daniel William Alexander. He had been a member of a group called simply, "The African Church". Some of its clergy decided to secede in October of 1923 and seek union with the African Orthodox Church in America. The new group was not immediately received, but after careful investigation, Alexander was named Bishop for the Province of South Africa. A clergyman who had been suspended by McGuire, the Reverend Edwin Urban Lewis attempted to create problems for the new union by reporting to the British Consul-General in New York, that the Province of South Africa had been created to make it easier for Marcus Garvey to obtain a visa to enter South Africa. Marcus Garvey never did visit South Africa and Lewis' information merely found its way to the Public Record Office in London.

Again, it is obvious that while Garvey was not a member of the AOC and while it had no organizational connection with the UNIA, he was interested in the new union. When Alexander's group met and decided to seek union with the AOC, Joseph Masogo the local agent for Garvey's <u>Negro World</u> was present both to observe and to give encouragement to the group's action.

The African Orthodox Church made some small progress in South Africa and, in addition, it played a role in the formation of several other independent churches throughout Africa. In 1925 Reuben Mukasa

Spartas, a Ugandan Anglican, who founded the African Progressive Association, contacted Bishop McGuire and expressed an interest in becoming part of the African Orthodox Church. Spartas was much influenced by the writings of Marcus Garvey and like Garvey's UNIA his own Association worked for similar ends and embraced similar ideals. After meeting with Alexander he formed a Ugandan African Orthodox Church. which remained only a short while with the African Orthodox Church. He was a long distance from South Africa and after a time he became uncertain about the Orthodoxy of Alexander and the South African Orthodox Church. He withdrew himself and the churches under his jurisdiction and went to Meletios II, the Greek Orthodox Patriarch of Alexandria and All Africa. He was received into full membership in 1946 and it was an occasion that set severral precedents. First, it was the first independent Black church to accept the authority of one of the historic episcopates, but more importantly, it was a church in the Vilatte Succession that was recognized and received by a historic Orthodox Church.

It was, however, in Kenya that the African Orthodox Church had its greatest success. The Kikuyus responded earlier to various Protestant missionaries, but soon found that although the Christian Faith appealed to them some of the European cultural attitudes did not. In 1929 many of them withdrew from the missions in an argument over female circumcision. Two new bodies were organized; the Kikuya Independent Schools Association and the Kikuyu Karling's Education Association. The Churches connected with the former mission schools were also a part of these new organizations, but there were few clergy to serve the churches. Archbishop Daniel Alexander was invited to Kenya and in 1935 he traveled throughout the land, preaching, and offereing the Sacraments. Before leaving he ordained four men. When he sailed away two years later he left behind him a solid church organization with native leadership capable of building the African Orthodox Church of Kenya. When Archbishop Makarios, the President of Cyprus, visited Kenya in 1971, in the course of a single weekend he personally baptized five thousand people into the African Orthodox Church. Before Archbishop Alexander's death on May 14, 1969, the AOC had established itself in Ghana and a number of independent churches were established throughout Africa either as a result of the example of the AOC or through the work of priests who had left the AOC. In all of these new churches there was the spirit of African nationalism. As African nations moved towards independence it seemed to many in the churches , that it was equally important that the churches have as its leaders members of the Black race. In most cases the churches achieved liberation before the nations in which they were located.

 Although race was the principal factor

in the emergence of the African Orthodox Church, and its related bodies, by no means is it a "racist" church. George Alexander McGuire in the first year of his episcopate visited His Holiness Melitios, the Ecomenical Patriarch to establish ties with the main body of the Orthodox Church. It is obvious from the report in "The Negro Churchman" of April 1923 that McGuire felt he had been promised full recognition, contingent on the continued growth and stability of the African Orthodox Church. The report of the visit and some subsequent events reads as follows: (1) "On December 30th, 1921, three months after our consecration to the episcopate, through the courtesy of the Russian Archbishop Alexander and the Greek Bishop Alexander Rodostolou, we were presented to His Holiness Melitios, Ecumenical Patriarch of the Orthodox Faith throughout the World We were received with brotherly love and the blessing of the Ecumenical Throne of Christendom was bestowed upon the work of the African Orthodox Church that it may fill the place designed for it, and becoem veritably, by the grace of God, and the devotion of its members, the restoration of the African Race of the Church established for them in the very days of the Apostles. Previous to

---

1. "Editorials: Our Interview with the Patriarch of Constantinople", THE NEGRO CHURCHMAN, April 1923, pages 1-2.

our consecration we had been favored with important conference with His Eminence Platon and Archbishop Alexander to discuss certain conditions under which the episcopate might be given us through Russian Orthodoxy. We were obliged to decline as we would be virtually a Mission rather than a Racial autonomous and autocephalous Church. When Patriarch Melitios inquired the origin of our episcopate and was told through his interpreter that it was from the Syrian Jacobite (Antioch) line of succession from the Apostle St. Peter, he pronounced it valid. He further inquired as to our Faith, especially to discover whether any trace of Monophysite teaching (which though not now held by the Jacobites:) had descended to us. We submitted copies of the Declaration of Faith of the African Orthodox Church, and having assured His Holiness that we rejected the Filioque of Western Christendom, that we held to the Seven Sacraments and acknowledge the authority of the Seven Ecumenical Councils of the Undivided Church, he declared us to be orthodox. Finally he sought and received information concerning the number of our clergy, churches, communicants and adherents. In turn, we desired of His Holiness to inform us what hope the African Orthodox Church might cherish of being given recognition in the Orthodox Communion. Indeed this was our main purpose in seeking the interview. His answer through his interpreter was as follows: "Since the Episcopate of the African Orthodox Church is from Eastern sources, and since you have accepted the

Orthodox Faith, you have only to extend your church among your Race, and when you shall have increased, and your ecclesiastical organization shall have shown stability, official recognition will be accorded you." And then he added this statement, which in the light of certain alleged recognition recently reported we are now able to understand, "Since we feel kindly disposed to those who are far removed from us, it is natural that we should feel more so towards you who have a share in our Orders and Faith." It is interesting to note in this connection that Archbishop Alexander extended us an invitation in our official capacity as Primate of the African Orthodox Church to be present at the Pontifical Eucharist celebrated at the Russian Cathedral of St. Nicholas by His Holiness the Patriarch of Constantinople assisted by otheer Prelates of the Orthodox Faith in America.

Although Archbishop McGuire was unable to attend the event, several of his clergy were present for the Patriarch's celebration of the Eucharist at the Cathedral of St. Nicholas. Recognition never followed. either because the AOC did not show the growth, or the stability that was required. A decade later it was to experience a schism that took several decades to heal. Another factor that may have played a role in the Church's failure to receive recognition, is its use of the Western Rite. At that time none of the Orthodox Churches in America had sanctioned the use of the Western Rite. When it was introduced several decades later it created a great storm of controversy. Further, the existing ethnic communions were not anxious to see another Orthodox jurisdiction in America, especially one for which there was no historical precedent.

Only the Russians were friendly to the AOC and shortly after McGuire's visit to Constantinople they released one of their priests, a monk, The Rev. Robert Hill, to service in the AOC. Unfortunately, he left a few months later to begin a schismatic group and the Russians participated in his deposition and excommunication which was conducted in the AOC Cathedral of the Good Shepherd.

Archbishop McGuire and his fellow members, while they saw their apostolate as being largely concerned with the fate and the souls of the members of their own race, not only sought to have the Church affiliated with Constantinople, but they also declared repeatedly that membership was open to men and women of all races. Anyone who has visited a congregation of the AOC is made to feel welcome regardless of his color or national background. Further the African Orthodox Church has ordained and consecrated a number of White men to serve as priests and bishops of White churches which were in communion with the AOC.

A clear example of its position manifested itself in 1928 when a schism developed in the American Catholic Church.

On January 8, 1928 a very unusual meeting took place at St. John's American Catholic Church in New York City. The pastor, Fr. Willian F. Tyarks served a mixed congregation that was largely Black. He informed the congregation that he had severed all connections with the American Catholic Church and therefore he felt it was necessary to resign as pastor. He told them that he planned to assist in the formation of a new Church, to be called the American Catholic Orthodox Church which would seek intercommunion with the African Orthodox Church. Further, the new Church, "would confine its activities entirely to members of the white race and to leave the people of African decent entirely to the African Orthodox Church in the conviction that this arrangement is both right, just, and fraternal".

Following his advice the congregation then voted unaminously to petition the AOC for membership and it was accepted on January 30, 1928. What was proprosed was that there would be two Orthodox Churches in the Vilatte line, one which would devote its efforts to minstering to Whites and one to Negroes. On January 14, the new American Catholic Orthodox Church had petitioned Archbishop McGuire to consecrate, by then, Bishop-elect Tyraks to head the new Church. Perhaps mindful of how long it took the AOC to find a White bishop to consecrate George McGuire, the AOC and Archbishop McGuire acted swiftly. On February 12, all the necessary investigation was completed and all the docu-

were signed, and Father William F. Tyarks was consecrated first bishop of the American Catholic Orthodox Church. Although the new Church never became very large it continued to enjoy close and fraternal relations with the AOC.

The African Orthodox Church entered into a similar agreement Archbishop Axel Z. Fryxell's jurisdiction in Chicago. At the Eleventh General Synod in September of 1931 it was voted to enter into an intercommunion with Bishop Fryxell's Church. It was also agreed that the AOC would care for the Blacks and Bishop Fryxell's jurisdiction would confine its ministry to Whites.

Relations with the American Catholic Church, headed by Archbishop Frederic E. J. Lloyd, continued to be very cordial, even though Bishop McGuire had consecrated Bishop Tyarks, who had defected from Lloyd's jurisdiction. A good example of the close communion between these two Vilatte jurisdictions, one Black and one White, can be studied in the founding of St. Matthew's African Orthodox Church in Chicago. The mission, which would play a large role in the growth and the extension of the African Orthodox Church, was the work of Robert Arthur Valentine, who was born in Antigua, B.W.I. on May 2, 1880. He graduated fro Moco College in Kingston, Jamaica and began his career as a teacher in 1902. Like many West Indian Negroes he was an active member of the Anglican Church and in time was licensed as a reader and received a Catechist's certificate from the

Jamaica Theological College. In 1918 he went to Montreal, Canada and worked in the office of the Auditor of Claims for the Canadian Pacific Railway Company. While in Canada he was active in a Congregational Church as superintendent of the Sunday School. He went to Chicago in 1922 and entered Moody Bible Institute. It is not known whether he heard of the African Orthodox Church while in Canada or while studying at Moody. It is probable that it was in Chicago where he began to subscribe to The Negro Churchman and began his correspondence with Archbishop George McGuire. Valentine was quickly attracted to the AOC because he had long since become disillusioned with the Protestant Episcopal Church and its treatment of its Negro members. Like most West Indians who had become accustomed to the better treatment of Negroes in the West Indian Anglican Church, he expected to be treated equally as well by the Episcopal Church in the United States. He quickly found that the average Episcopal parish would welcome a single Negro with warmth and enthusiasm, but two Negroes with less warmth and no enthusiasm. Larger numbers, he found, were decidedly unwelcome.

In the African Orthodox Church he saw an opportunity to serve in a Church not dominated by Whites and dedicated to the improvement of the Negro Race. He also found it easy to relate to +George A. McGuire, as a fellow West Indian and to the West Indian flavor of the Church as a whole. He quickly resolved to cast his lot with the AOC and when Archbishop McGuire arranged for his further studies under Archbishop Frederick Lloyd, he agreed with alacrity. He did not fail to note that Archbishop Lloyd, now sixty-five years of age, had had an illustrious career in the Episcopal Church, as well as heading the American Catholic Church for several decades, held Archbishop McGuire in very high regard. Thus it was possible for a Negro Churchman to be part of an autocephalous Orthodox Body and command the respect of other churhmen. On September 21, 1924 at the request of Archbishop McGuire, Robert Arthur Valentine was ordained to the subdiaconate in St. Cecelia's Chapel, ACC, by Archbishop Lloyd

Archbishop McGuire was aware of the potential of his new deacon and he gave him his full support in the undertaking of the Chicago mission. In January of the following year he gave permission for the organization of St. Matthew's Mission and again employed the good services of Archbishop Lloyd. Eleven people signed the roll and Archbishop Lloyd signed as witness. The Church would grow under the leadership of Valentine, who in May 1925 was ordained a priest by the Primate, George Alexander McGuire. On May 30, 1930 he was consecrated a bishop of the African Orthodox Church. St. Matthew's grew and prospered until the 1950's when it began to decline with Bishop Valentine's advancing age.

## UNTO THE FOUR CORNERS OF THE WORLD

As one reads through the issues of The Negro Churchman from 1923 through 1931, one has to marvel at the ability of Archbishop George McGuire to concern himself with the many places where the Church reached out and took root. The first issue appeared in January of 1923 under editorship of Archbishop McGure. He not only edited it, but he served as business manager as well, and wrote a good deal of the material which appeared in it.

In the first issue, which was published only sixteen months after the Church's founding, of the ten clergy, four served outside of the United States, namely in Cuba, Haiti, and Canada. He was not content to adminster the foreign Churches from his New York office, but in spite of the limited resources of the Church in July of 1923 he traveled through New England, visiting Churches there and then went on to St. Philip's Church in Sydney, Nova Scotia. When he returned, however, he could see that the Church was spread too widely geographically to have but one bishop. At the Third General Synod, The

The Rev. William E. Robertson was elected to the episcopate. Father Robertson was pastor of St. Luke's Church in Cambridge, Massachusetts and it was clear that St. Luke's would become a strong Church in the AOC.

At the same synod it was voted to tax every member twenty-five cents a year for the Church Extension Fund. The amount may appear small today, but in 1923 it represented much more considering the wages and the economic disadvantages of the AOC's Negro members. Perhaps one reason for the willingness of the delegates to tax themselves was the receipt of a petition from The Rev. H.S.A. Hartley of Port of Spain, Trinidad, B.W.I. He and his small Moravian congregation were asking the AOC to receive them into membership Their petition as accepted and one hundred dollars was subscribed to pay the passage of the Rev. Dixon Philips, the AOC's missionary in Trinidad, to New York so that he could report on the work there and raise funds for church extension. Of course, it was not a steady forward march, for often the Church had to abandon projects begun earlier with great hope. In the same issue of The Negro Churchman, we note the disappearance of the work in Haiti.

The new bishop was consecrated in November following the Synod, by Archbishop Frederick Lloyd, as the chief consecrator. Interestingly, a bull allowing this consecration was received from

Archbishop Joseph Rene Vilatte, who was at this time, retired at the Abbey of Pont-Colbert, a Cistercian Abbey near Versailles. He had presumably submitted to the Papacy but evidently felt enough affection for the AOC, which he helped to create, to break his agreement not to function as a bishop, in order to issue this bull. By December of 1923 we note a large increase in the number of parishes and clergy and the extension of the Church to New Orleans and to Chicago. Also we note a new bishop had been consecrated for Canada, the Right Rev. Arthur Stanley Trotman. The consecration took place September 10, 1924 at the Church of the Good Shepherd and the consecrating bishops were both of the African Orthodox Church, namely, Bishops McGuire and Robertson. At this time, Bishop McGuire was raised to the position of Archbishop.

The first extension of the Church to Africa took place on January 1, 1925 when the First Provincial Synod of South Africa was opened in the Church of St. Augustine of Hippo, Beaconsfield, Griqualand West. They synod declared itself to be the African orthodox of South Africa and in communion with the African Orthodox Church in America. They chose Daniel W. Alexander as their Archbishop-Elect. The Church accepted the Declaration of Faith of the AOC, The Divine Liturgy, and a local adaptation of the Constitution and Canons of the AOC. They had hoped to to be received by the Fifth Synod of the Church which met in New York City in September of that year. However, the

AOC was cautious and voted to accept the South African Church as a Mission Territory. The action was well received in South Africa as the people there saw the reasonableness of a probationary period in the light of the distance between Africa and America.

In the next year the Archbishop would have to deal with both growth and problems at home. The Church was reaching into Florida and was prospering. The rapid growth in the state was not without problems and after one controversay some dissidents left and were received by Archbishop Lloyd into the American Catholic Church. Since it had been agreed that the ACC would confine its work to the White population and the AOC would serve the Negroes, the AOC at its Fifth General Synod severed all relations with the American Catholic Church. At the same synod word was heard of the progress of the AOC in the Dominican Republic, and of the training of its priests at its Endich Theological Seminary. The seminary, at this time, had fourteen resident students and four receiving courses through the extension service. Because of the growth in the United States, Fr. Reginald Grant Barrow, a native of Barbados, was consecrated as Bishop of Long Island on the 8th of September by the three African Orthodox bishops, George A. McGuire, William Ernest Robertson, and Arthur Stanley Trotman.

Archbishop McGuire soon discovered that

he could not longer find sufficient time for his many labors nor the energy. As a physician, he realized that there were physical limitations which he must not overstep. He had in 1924 suffered a physical collaspe but unfortunately he did not heed the warning. On Sunday, May 2, 1926 after celebrating Mass at the Cathedral Church of St. Peter in Miami, he again collapsed and only the early arrival of medical help saved his life. In the June issue of The Negro Churchman there appeared his letter of resignation and he set sail for Bermuda for a few weeks of rest and recuperation. The resignation sent shock waves throughout the Church and letters poured in begging him to reconsider. Archbishop McGuire did heed these pleas and after getting another medical opinion, he withdrew his resignation and decided to serve a while longer. He stated at the Extraordinary Meeting of the General Synod which convened in Christ Church Cathedral, Booklyn, on Septpember 1, 1926 that he suffered merely from, "an excessive increase of adipose tissue", i.e. bishop's syndrome. He set about to correct this problem with his usual determination and energy and quickly returned to health. He did, however, distribute some of his heavy burden to the other bishops. Bishop Willian Robertson was given the administration of the new work in Nicarauga and Bishop Reginal Barrow was given the supervision of the work in South Africa.

 The Church in South Africa had chosen its leadership well and the Archbishop-Elect was able to report substantial growth in membership and in the number of clergy. It is interesting to note where the clergy were coming from, it it is as McGuire envisioned, a bringing together of Negroes from various denominations to unite in the African Orthodox Church. Fr. Alexander reported, "We have recently gained four spledid clergymen, Fr. Damane, formerly a Romanist; Fr. Morgan, formerly Swedendborgian  Fr. Dithebe, formerly Anglican, and Rev. S. Daniels, formerly Wesleyan."

It is a tribute to the piety, the skill and the charisma of Archbishop McGuire, that the Church continued to grow and experienced no schism during his lifetime. Whenhe died in 1934 he left behind a strong and vigorous Church, not only in the United States, but in the British West Indies, and in Africa. In Kenya there are over a million adherents who either belong to the African Orthodox Church or one of the several offshoots from it. The Church in the United States today is presented by two branches, the African Orthodox Church with headquarters in New York and the African Orthodox Church of the West, with headquarters in Chicago. Most of the parishes in the East date back to McGuire's time. The parishes in the West are more recent and have been the results of the work of Archbishop G. Duncan Hinkson, a native of the Barbados who has both a theological and a medical training.

But whether in the East or the West, the African Orthodox Church has since its founding remained faithful to Orthodoxy and brought dignity and spiritual strength to the Race which founded it and which it continues to serve in the spirit of Christ.

ARCHBISHOP GEORGE ALEXANDER McGUIRE, D. D , M. D
Begins the Eleventh Year of his Consecration placing his Chair
In Holy Cross Pro-Cathedral Church.

## BIBLIOGRAPHY

Bragg, George F., Jr.  "History of the Afro-American Group of the Episcopal Church", Baltimore; Church Advocate Press, 1922, 319 pp

Burkett, Randall K. and Richard Newman, editors  "Black Apostles", Boston: G. K. Hall & Co., 1978, 283 pp

Burkett, Randall K.  "Black Redemption", Philadelphia: Temple University Press, 1978, 197 pp

————  "Garveyism as a Religious Movement", Metuchen, NJ: Scarecrow Press, 1978, 216 pp

Garvey, Amy Jacques  "Garvey & Garveyism", New York: The Macmillan Co., 1970, 336 pp

Levine, Lawrence W. "Marcus Garvey and the Politics of Revitalization", pages 105-138 (of) "Black Leaders of the Twentieth Century", edited by John Hope Franklin and August Meier, Urvan, IL: University of Illinois Press, 1982, 372 pp

Pruter, Karl and J. Gordon Melton "The Old Catholic Sourcebook", New York: Garland Publishing, 1983, 254 pp

Wilmore, Gayraud S. "Black Religion and Black Radicalism", Maryknoll, NY: Orbis Books, 1983, 288 pp

Young, Henry J. "Major Black Religious Leaders 1755-1940", Nashville: Abingdon, 1977, 173 pp

Periodicals

""""The Negro Churchman", Volumes 1-9, 1923-1931, Reprinted with Introductory Essay by Richard Newman, Millwood, NY: Kraus Reprint Co. 1977 2 volumes

www.ingramcontent.com/pod-product-compliance
Lightning Source LLC
LaVergne TN
LVHW041459070426
835507LV00009B/690